Contributors

BIGFOOT
B.T. POLCARI
DAN EHL
DAVID MEMMOLI
DAVID KEYES
DONNA BESEL
CE HUNTINGDON
IDALITA WRIGHT RASO
JASON BEHNKE
KATHY HAYNES
KISANE SLANEY
L. J. AMBROSIO
MIKE WEEDALL
PATRICIA BOSSANO
RHEA THOMAS
RICK S. SULIK
ROBERT JAFFEE
STEPHEN WEINSTOCK
TIMOTHY JAY SMITH

Review Tales
A Book Magazine For Indie Authors

Founder & Editor in Chief: S. Jeyran Main
Publisher: Review Tales Publishing & Editing Services
Print & Distribution: Ingram Spark
Designs: Pexels
ISBN 978-1-988680-83-5 (Paperback)
ISBN 978-1-988680-82-8 (Digital)
www.jeyranmain.com
For all inquiries, please contact us directly.

Photo Credits from Pexels:
pexels-olly-3755760
pexels-gabby-k-5634667
pexels-eugene-golovesov-1810803-29196409

Editor's Note

Welcome to the 10th edition of Review Tales Magazine!

Reaching double digits feels like a milestone moment—a turning point in any good story where the characters realize how far they've come, yet also how much possibility still lies ahead. For us, this moment is both thrilling and humbling. What began as a small effort to give books and authors a platform has grown into a community, a conversation, and, I dare say, a movement that continues to celebrate the power of storytelling.

This achievement would not have been possible without the incredible authors who entrusted us with their work. Your courage to share your words, your creativity to shape them, and your commitment to seeing them through are what keep the literary world vibrant. Every page you write sparks conversation, stirs reflection, and reminds us all why books remain the most enduring kind of magic.

To our readers, writers, and supporters—you are the heartbeat of this magazine. Whether you come here to discover your next favorite book, learn from the journeys of fellow authors, or revel in the joy of good literature, your loyalty has carried us here. Each edition is a collaboration with you, and your encouragement fuels our ongoing efforts to raise the bar continually.

As we celebrate this 10th edition, our mission remains steady: to review with thoughtfulness, to feature with intention, and to champion authors at every stage of their creative path. Yet, we also look forward—with fresh ideas, new voices, and the determination to keep making this magazine a place where both authors and readers feel seen, heard, and inspired.

As you turn these pages, I invite you to immerse yourself in stories, insights, and voices that truly matter. May you find encouragement to start—or finish—your own next chapter, and may you continue to walk alongside us as we set our sights on the next ten editions and beyond.

Here's to the journeys still waiting to be written, and to the joy of sharing them together.

With gratitude and a dash of wit,

Jeyran Main

Jeyran Main
Editor-in-Chief
Review Tales Magazine

FALL 2025 | ISSUE 10

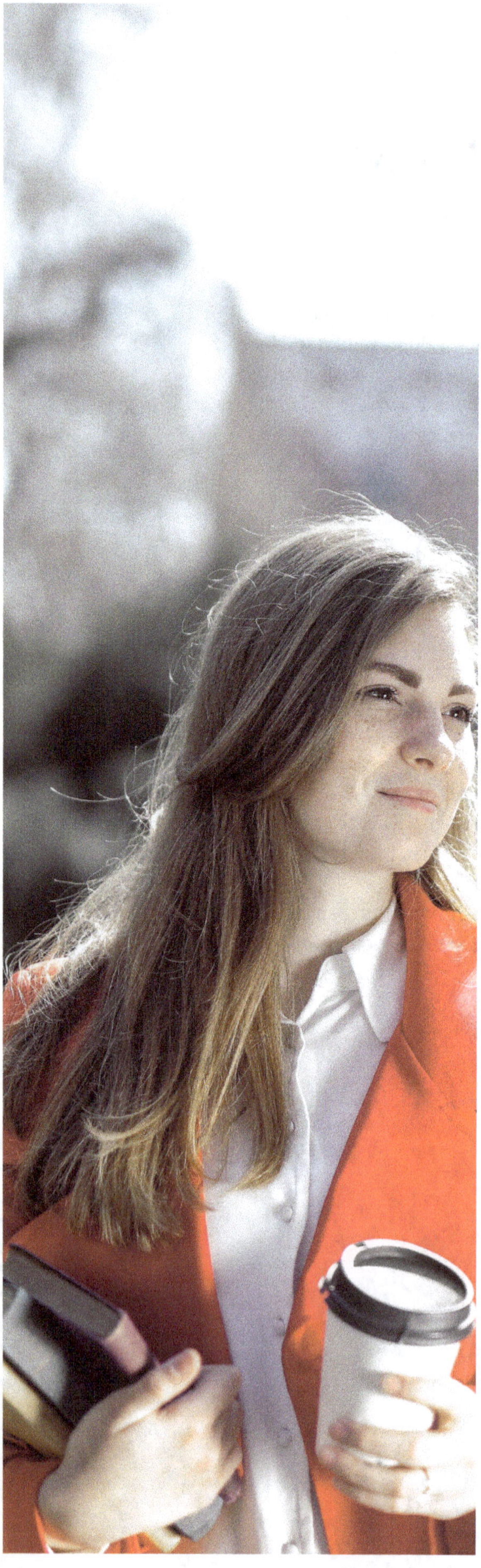

BOOK REVIEWS

Review Tales is thrilled to have reached the milestone of over 2000 book reviews. With this extensive experience, we've had the privilege of exploring a vast range of literature. Our reviews are always impartial and thoughtfully crafted to highlight authors' strengths while inspiring them to keep creating. For this summer issue, we've handpicked exceptional book reviews to feature.

TO APPLY FOR A BOOK REVIEW VISIT
WWW.JEYRANMAIN.COM

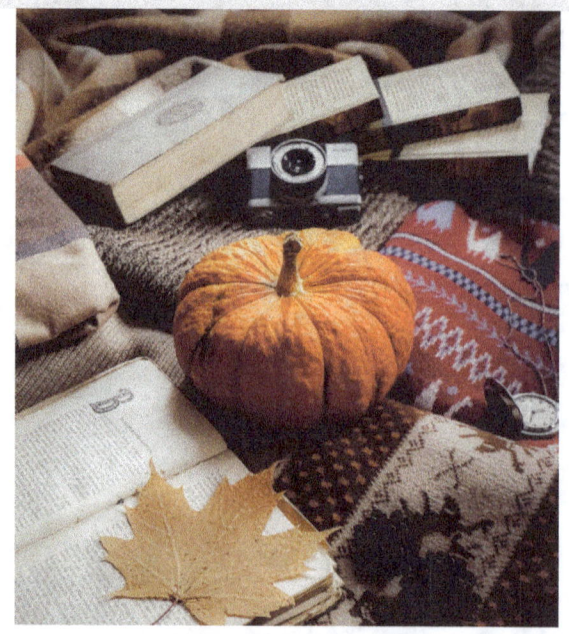

Book Reviews

CHILDREN OF THE FIRE MOON
Bigfoot

Reviewer: Jeyran Main

Children of the Fire Moon by Bigfoot is a short, imaginative journey that straddles the line between dark fantasy and sci-fi adventure. With its whimsical yet eerie setting on a distant moon, the book introduces readers to Robert, Margo, and Jimi, three young characters navigating a world entirely alien to our own. From the opening pages, Bigfoot immerses readers in the strange and mysterious environment of the Swamble's cave, inviting them to explore alongside the protagonists in a place where the rules of Earthly life do not apply.

What immediately stands out in Children of the Fire Moon is its playful reimagining of the coming-of-age story. The children live without the markers of everyday human experience—no birthdays, no chocolate, no parental guidance, and even the simple act of brushing their teeth is foreign to them. This choice by the author amplifies the sense of isolation and otherworldliness, while simultaneously providing a unique lens through which to examine growth, friendship, and discovery. For readers aged ten to ninety-nine, the book offers a layered experience: younger readers can delight in the adventure and fantastical setting, while older readers may appreciate the subtle commentary on the nature of learning, independence, and curiosity.

Bigfoot's prose is compact yet evocative, creating a world that feels vast despite the story's brevity. The narrative is direct and uncomplicated, making it accessible to a wide range of readers, while also carrying enough intrigue and strangeness to keep adults engaged. The plot moves swiftly, never lingering too long on exposition, which is particularly effective given the story's short format.

The book also excels in its imaginative approach to storytelling. The distant moon setting is vividly constructed, from the peculiar Swamble's cave to the strange customs and routines—or lack thereof —that define the children's lives. Robert, Margo, and Jimi are endearing in their curiosity and resilience, and their interactions bring both humor and tension to the narrative. Bigfoot balances moments of suspense with whimsical oddities, creating a reading experience that is unpredictable yet coherent, keeping readers invested in the characters' journey and the mysteries of their world.

Children of the Fire Moon blends elements of fantasy, sci-fi, and dark whimsy to create a story that is both entertaining and thought-provoking. The book encourages readers to consider how experience, environment, and imagination shape identity, while providing plenty of adventure and intrigue along the way.

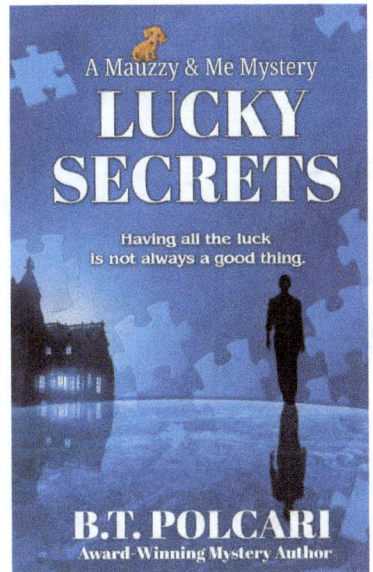

LUCKY SECRETS
B.T. Polcari

Reviewer: Jeyran Main

Lucky Secrets by B.T. Polcari is a thrilling addition to the Mauzzy & Me series, delivering suspense, intrigue, and a fast-paced narrative that keeps readers on the edge of their seats. As the third installment in the series, this novel follows college student Sara Donovan, who finds herself reluctantly drawn into a mysterious contest with high stakes and even higher tension. The story opens with a sense of foreboding as Sara receives an unexpected package containing an invitation to an exclusive contest, accompanied by unsettling photographs and a threatening note that leaves no room for refusal.

The author does an excellent job of combining mystery and psychological tension, as Sara must navigate not only the elaborate puzzles of the contest but also the underlying threats that target her personal history. Each of the eight other contestants carries their own secrets, creating a web of suspicion and intrigue that keeps both Sara and the reader guessing. The inclusion of seven complex levels of riddles and puzzles adds a clever interactive element to the narrative, making the story feel like a game in which readers can imagine themselves participating, heightening engagement and suspense. The challenges are both inventive and challenging, allowing Polcari to demonstrate creativity while building tension in each stage of the contest.

Polcari's characterization of Sara is strong and relatable; her determination, intelligence, and resourcefulness anchor the story amidst the chaos of the contest and its dark undertones. The tension escalates effectively with the discovery of a contestant's body, which forces Sara to confront the possibility of danger and raises the stakes beyond mere competition. The author balances the suspense with moments of reflection and strategic thinking, highlighting Sara's problem-solving skills and resilience under pressure.

The mansion setting serves as both glamorous and ominous, providing a perfect backdrop for a high-stakes game where appearances are deceiving, and trust is scarce. Polcari's prose is concise and gripping, ensuring that the plot moves briskly without sacrificing the atmospheric buildup or the depth of mystery. The mix of luxury and danger within the mansion walls enhances the story's tension and emphasizes the contrast between outward elegance and hidden peril.

Lucky Secrets explores themes of courage, secrecy, and survival in a contest where nothing is as it seems. With its blend of puzzles, danger, and complex character dynamics, the book provides readers with an engaging and suspenseful experience, ideal for fans of mystery and contemporary thriller adventures.

JAK BARLEY, PRIVATE INQUISITOR, AND THE CASE OF ABSENTMINDFULLNESS

Dan Ehl

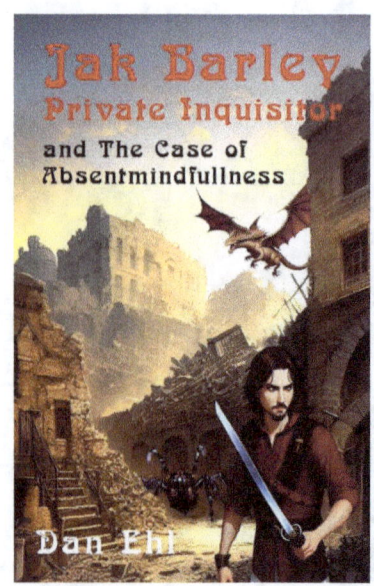

Reviewer: Jeyran Main

Jak Barley, Private Inquisitor, and The Case of Absentmindfullness by Dan Ehl is an inventive and action-packed finale to the Jak Barley series, blending mystery, dark humor, and fantasy elements into a uniquely engaging narrative. As the ninth installment, the book follows the resourceful and irreverent private inquisitor Jak Barley, whose latest case is anything but ordinary. From the first page, readers are drawn into a world where danger lurks in every shadow, and nothing is as straightforward as it seems. The story begins with Jak investigating an asylum where patients appear to be in zombie-like states, immediately setting a tone of eerie suspense mixed with absurdity.

Ehl excels at crafting intricate plots that seamlessly interweave multiple storylines. Jak's investigation quickly escalates when he is approached by a hivemind swarm of bees demanding that he locate their kidnapped queen. This unusual case merges the fantastical with the detective genre, showcasing the author's creativity and humor. The tension intensifies as hired assassins enter the scene, threatening Jak's life while adding layers of intrigue and suspense. A seemingly simple free passage on a cruise ship turns perilous as murder, conspiracies, and secretive elite factions intersect, creating a labyrinthine plot that keeps readers guessing at every turn.

The mythical suit of armor hidden in lost fortress ruins introduces a compelling magical element, with vying wizard cabals adding stakes and complexity to the narrative. Jak's interactions with supporting characters, including the enigmatic Witch Morgana and his alternate-world friend Lorenzo Spasm, add depth and humor to the story, offering readers both emotional resonance and comic relief. Ehl's world-building is imaginative and detailed, blending elements of noir, urban fantasy, and mystery into a cohesive and immersive setting.

The pacing is brisk, expertly balancing action sequences, investigative work, and character-driven moments. Jak's wit and irreverence provide levity amid high-stakes situations, ensuring that tension never overwhelms the humor and charm that define the series. Ehl's prose is sharp and engaging, drawing readers into a narrative that is as unpredictable as it is entertaining.

Jak Barley, Private Inquisitor, and The Case of Absentmindfullness is a satisfying conclusion to a series that thrives on originality, humor, and suspense. With a complex plot, imaginative world-building, and memorable characters, it offers readers a thrilling adventure where mystery, magic, and mayhem collide in unexpected ways, keeping fans enthralled from start to finish.

STARTING YOUR OWN BUSINESS
David Memmoli

Reviewer: Jeyran Main

Starting Your Own Business by David Memmoli is a comprehensive, all-in-one guide designed to help aspiring entrepreneurs navigate the complexities of launching and managing a successful business. This course-style program stands out for its integration of multiple learning formats, ensuring that students with varied preferences—visual, auditory, and hands-on—can fully engage with the material. At its core, the program combines two virtual textbooks, Business Fundamentals and Advanced Concepts, providing a solid foundation and a deeper dive into sophisticated business strategies. Each textbook comes with an interactive companion workbook, which allows readers to apply concepts in real-time, strengthening retention and practical understanding.

Memmoli's approach is uniquely structured, pairing the textbooks with audio versions in both male and female voices, catering to auditory learners and those who prefer on-the-go learning. This flexibility ensures that the content is accessible and digestible, allowing students to revisit key concepts at their own pace. The inclusion of summary PowerPoints reinforces core ideas, providing a convenient review tool and a quick reference guide for essential business principles.

The program's instructional course is expansive and interactive, with a dedicated module for each textbook. These courses guide students step by step through practical exercises, business simulations, and strategic decision-making processes. By actively engaging learners in real-world scenarios, Memmoli helps bridge the gap between theoretical knowledge and practical application, which is critical for anyone preparing to launch a business.

Purchasing the $500 course also grants a one-year free subscription to the Another Way Business website, offering additional resources, tools, and ongoing support. This feature emphasizes the program's commitment to long-term success and continuous learning, making it a valuable investment for new entrepreneurs.

Overall, Starting Your Own Business provides a holistic, immersive, and practical experience. Memmoli's methodical yet flexible approach ensures that readers not only understand the fundamental principles of business but are also equipped to implement them effectively. With its combination of textbooks, workbooks, audio guides, instructional courses, and digital resources, this program is ideal for aspiring business owners seeking a structured and interactive path to entrepreneurial success.

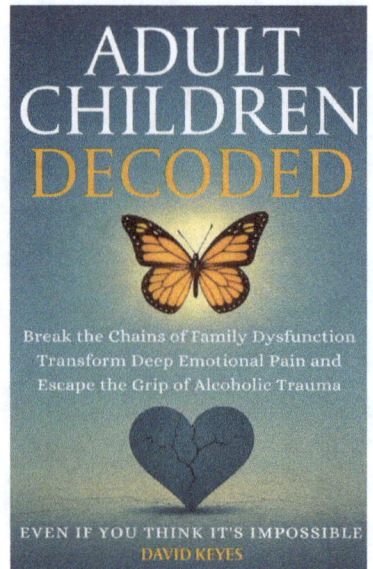

ADULT CHILDREN DECODED
David Keyes

Reviewer: Jeyran Main

Adult Children Decoded: Break the Chains of Family Dysfunction, Transform Deep Emotional Pain, and Escape the Grip of Alcoholic Trauma—Even If You Don't Believe It's Possible by David Keyes is an essential guide for anyone seeking to heal from the deep emotional wounds inflicted by dysfunctional or alcoholic families. With an intimate and empathetic voice, Keyes navigates readers through the complex terrain of childhood trauma, showing how these early experiences continue to shape adult life, relationships, and self-perception.

What sets this book apart is its blending of personal narrative with practical guidance. Keyes draws on his own life experiences, from surviving PTSD after serving in Iraq to enduring an abusive marriage, to illustrate the profound impact that unresolved trauma can have. These stories are not only compelling but serve as bridges for readers who may see reflections of their own struggles in his experiences. The author's vulnerability builds trust, making the book both relatable and deeply human.

The book's structure is thoughtfully designed to combine insight with action. Readers are guided through strategies to understand the patterns of family dysfunction, recognize the emotional chains that hold them back, and adopt tools for healing and empowerment. The inclusion of modern recovery approaches alongside real-life examples from other adult children of dysfunctional families enhances the educational value, offering multiple pathways toward emotional freedom.

Keyes emphasizes that healing is not linear, but possible. His guidance addresses a wide spectrum of issues, including strained family dynamics, the effects of emotional neglect, and the specific challenges faced by those who grew up in alcoholic households. Through this approach, he reframes trauma not as a life sentence but as a challenge that can be understood, managed, and ultimately overcome.

The book's compassionate tone, paired with actionable advice, ensures that it resonates with a broad audience, whether readers are beginning their healing journey or looking for ways to strengthen existing recovery practices. By focusing on both understanding and empowerment, Adult Children Decoded provides a practical and hopeful roadmap for reclaiming emotional well-being, enhancing relationships, and cultivating self-worth.

This book is an invaluable resource for adult children seeking clarity, support, and guidance in escaping the grip of past pain and creating a healthier, more confident future.

THE UNRAVELLING
Donna Besel

Reviewer: Jeyran Main

Donna Besel's The Unravelling is a profoundly moving and unflinching memoir that explores the devastating consequences of sexual abuse within a family. The narrative begins at what should have been a joyful occasion—a sister's wedding in 1992—when the horrifying truth of their father, Jock Tod's, long-standing abuse is revealed. This disclosure leads to an overwhelming cascade of confessions, as Besel's five sisters admit they, too, had been assaulted. The book is both a personal testimony and a broader exploration of the ripple effects that abuse has on families and communities.

One of the most compelling aspects of Besel's writing is her courage in addressing the long-term emotional, psychological, and physical tolls of incest. She does not shy away from the painful realities, illustrating how trauma infiltrates every aspect of life: trust, relationships, and even one's sense of self. Her honesty allows readers to grasp the complexity of survivor experiences, beyond the initial act of abuse, highlighting the enduring challenges of navigating memory, shame, and fear.

Besel also provides a meticulous account of the legal process, from reporting the abuse to the protracted prosecution of her father. Through this lens, readers gain insight into the systemic obstacles victims often face in seeking justice, including skepticism from authorities, procedural delays, and societal judgment. This component of the book is particularly illuminating for anyone seeking to understand the intersection of personal trauma and the criminal justice system.

The writing is clear, deliberate, and empathetic, balancing narrative intimacy with educational insight. The memoir's impact is amplified by Besel's reflective commentary on resilience, strength, and the difficult journey toward healing. It is not merely a story of despair; it is also an examination of survival and the human capacity to confront unimaginable hardship while maintaining integrity and hope.

The Unravelling is essential reading for those interested in memoirs, social justice, and the psychological effects of abuse. Donna Besel's narrative is a brave, necessary, and profoundly human story that both educates and resonates, offering a rare window into the endurance of survivors and the complexities of reclaiming life after trauma.

ELLEN IN PUZANTIUM
CE Huntingdon

Reviewer: Jeyran Main

Ellen in Puzantium is a whimsical, offbeat fantasy that bursts with imagination, humor, and absurdity. The story follows Ellen, a quirky two-foot-four heroine with a lisp, who is unexpectedly thrust into a fantastical world where cats run buffets, snails are Saints, and prophecy is signaled by massive bowl cuts. Already struggling with the everyday challenges of life—such as putting her clothes on correctly and speaking clearly—Ellen must navigate the chaotic land of Puzantium and attempt to save it from a world-ending famine.

What makes this story stand out is its wildly inventive setting. CE Huntingdon combines classic fantasy tropes with absurd, almost surreal humor, creating a world where the mundane becomes extraordinary. The narrative is punctuated by clever gags, including thefts of the Abbot's pens, prank calls, and misadventures involving laxatives, all of which illustrate the playful tone that runs throughout the book. Ellen's misfit companions, particularly the elderly Brothers of Geriatric Abbey, add both warmth and comic relief, their loyalty and idiosyncrasies making them memorable characters in this fantastical romp.

Narratively, the story is told through the perspective of a talking dog, an inventive choice that adds a unique voice and perspective to the tale. This canine narrator not only provides humorous commentary but also grounds the chaos in a thread of consistency and charm, making the absurd plot surprisingly coherent. With over 100 illustrations, the book's visual elements complement the text, enhancing the immersive experience and bringing the quirky world of Puzantium vividly to life.

Beyond humor, Ellen in Puzantium explores themes of self-discovery, courage, and friendship, cleverly wrapped in zany antics and unconventional adventures. Ellen's journey is one of growth and reluctant heroism, showing that even the most unlikely characters can rise to challenges when faced with absurd odds.

This book is perfect for readers who enjoy whimsical fantasy, surreal humor, and energetic, fast-paced adventures. CE Huntingdon delivers a lofi, ADHD-fueled tale that celebrates the absurd and finds joy in the unpredictable. Ellen in Puzantium is both a laughter-filled escape and a charming story of resilience, imagination, and the magic hidden in everyday chaos.

EYE OF SATURN
Idalita Wright Raso

Reviewer: Jeyran Main

Eye of Saturn is an ambitious, dark fantasy that blends vampire mythology, historical intrigue, and epic adventure into a sweeping tale that spans continents and centuries. The story continues the saga of Felipe de Hayos, an undead lamsivetalak—a vampire cursed by his wife, the Immortal High Priestess Zaybeth—to walk the Earth for 550 years. With the opening of the Eye of Saturn approaching, Felipe must confront both mortal and supernatural adversaries while racing against time to free Zaybeth from the Netherworld.

Raso's novel excels in worldbuilding, merging historical events with fantastical elements in a seamless, immersive narrative. Set against the backdrop of 15th-century Wallachia, readers witness Felipe's involvement in the power struggles between Vlad Dracula III and the Ottoman Sultan Mehmed II. The stakes are heightened as Felipe assumes Dracula's likeness, navigating the legend of the vampire while fighting to preserve Wallachia's freedom. Raso enriches the tale with the Brethren of the Occultus Facultas—mystical monks armed with the Philosopher's Stone—introducing elements of alchemy and occult lore that deepen the story's mythos.

The novel's scope extends beyond European history into the New World, where Felipe encounters the horrors of slavery, demonstrating Raso's willingness to explore the darker dimensions of humanity alongside supernatural conflicts. Felipe's journey is both heroic and tragic, underscoring themes of love, loyalty, and sacrifice. His internal struggles—balancing his vampiric instincts with his moral compass—add depth to his character and invite readers to contemplate the cost of immortality.

Raso's writing is vivid and cinematic, with action sequences, political intrigue, and supernatural confrontations unfolding in a fast-paced, gripping style. The novel's combination of historical accuracy, mythic storytelling, and dark fantasy creates a layered reading experience that will appeal to fans of vampires, historical fiction, and epic adventures.

Eye of Saturn is a thrilling, complex continuation of a vampire epic, offering both high-stakes adventure and emotional resonance. Readers who enjoy vampire lore entwined with history, mystical intrigue, and morally complex heroes will find this sequel a compelling and unforgettable journey "Between Heaven and Saturn."

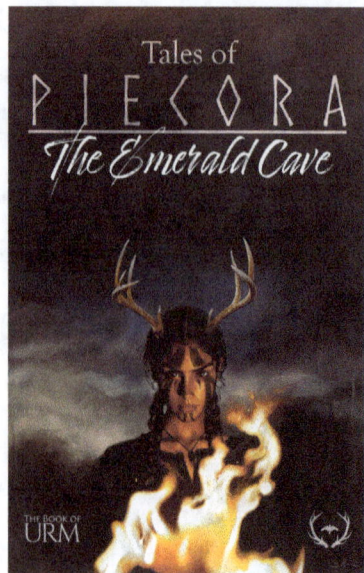

TALES OF PIECORA
Jason Behnke

Reviewer: Jeyran Main

The Emerald Cave, the first installment in Jason Behnke's Tales of Piecora series, is a vivid, high-stakes fantasy adventure that combines clever worldbuilding with compelling characters and a richly layered narrative. The story follows Serpendis Endium, a grizzled Master Merchant from Kannoniah and the sole survivor of a disastrous expedition into the unmappable Wildlands. While Serpendis longs for little more than the comfort of home, his journey takes a dramatic turn when he crosses paths with Piecora Tiorold, an expert Sienjan Guide whose skills are essential for survival in the chaotic Wildlands—even if he despises her at first.

The narrative quickly escalates when Serpendis discovers a forbidden cave containing cursed emeralds, plunging him and Piecora into a perilous adventure that spans multiple realities. Behnke skillfully weaves together elements of self-discovery, friendship, and moral courage, as the protagonists are forced to navigate a dangerous landscape while facing a powerful sorceress whose mastery of intentional interdimensional travel threatens the Undying Lands of the Eldar. The stakes are immense, and the journey is anything but predictable, making the story a gripping page-turner from start to finish.

One of the novel's strongest points is its rich characterization. Serpendis is a wonderfully flawed protagonist—curmudgeonly, self-interested, yet capable of growth and loyalty—while Piecora serves as a resourceful, resilient counterpart who drives the narrative forward with her intelligence and expertise. Their dynamic adds depth and humor to the story, balancing the tension of the unfolding adventure.

Behnke's worldbuilding is equally impressive. The Wildlands are chaotic and dangerous, the Undying Lands of the Eldar are vividly imagined, and the concept of reality-hopping adds layers of intrigue and unpredictability. Combined with the compelling narrative and inventive magic system, the novel immerses readers in a fantastical universe that feels both expansive and alive.

Tales of Piecora 01: The Emerald Cave is an exhilarating introduction to a series filled with adventure, danger, and discovery. Behnke delivers a story that will appeal to fans of epic fantasy, intricate worldbuilding, and character-driven narratives, promising an exciting continuation in the second book of the Book of Urm series.

THE MISSING YEARS
Kathy Haynes

Reviewer: Jeyran Main

Kathy Haynes' The Missing Years is a compelling and emotionally resonant exploration of family secrets, personal growth, and the search for identity. The novel follows Norah, a divorced, fatherless woman navigating adulthood with a sense of independence yet carrying the lingering scars of a complicated childhood. Despite her achievements and self-assured exterior, Norah struggles with trust, particularly in romantic relationships, shaped by the absence of her father and the instability it caused.

The story takes a transformative turn when Norah meets Allen and allows herself to open up to love. His sudden departure, however, triggers an emotional crisis, prompting her to follow her therapist's advice to redirect her focus. Norah chooses to create a digital scrapbook from her childhood photos—a decision that becomes both therapeutic and revelatory. This act of reflection uncovers long-buried memories, including visits to Dammasch, a mental health facility where she was forced to see her father at age thirteen. These memories serve as both haunting reminders and guiding clues, compelling her to confront a past she has long avoided.

Haynes's writing skillfully balances suspense, emotional depth, and character introspection. Norah's journey is not simply about uncovering her father's fate; it is a profound exploration of identity, resilience, and the intricate ways family shapes who we become. Her interactions with her family, who are reluctant to revisit painful truths, highlight the tension between secrecy and the need for closure, adding layers of complexity to the narrative.

The novel's pacing is thoughtful, allowing readers to immerse themselves in Norah's reflective process, while the emotional stakes maintain a compelling momentum. The story also thoughtfully examines the impact of unresolved trauma, the struggle to trust, and the courage required to pursue answers that may unsettle long-held beliefs.

The Missing Years is ultimately a poignant and introspective journey of self-discovery, where the quest to understand one's past becomes the key to embracing the future. Kathy Haynes delivers a deeply human narrative that resonates with anyone who has sought to reconcile love, loss, and family secrets. It is a novel that lingers, encouraging readers to consider how the echoes of our past shape the people we become.

THE HEIRESS
Kisane Slaney

Reviewer: Jeyran Main

Kisane Slaney's The Heiress is a sweeping, emotionally charged romance set against the vibrant backdrop of 1970s London and international intrigue. The novel tells the story of Tiana Manning, a young woman blessed with beauty, intelligence, and wealth, yet burdened by a secret love that could jeopardize everything she holds dear. From her first encounter with Father Philippe Gagnon in Paris to the rekindling of feelings years later, Tiana's journey is one of courage, passion, and personal growth.

What sets this romance apart is its compelling blend of heartfelt emotion and adventurous plot. Tiana's love for Philippe, who has devoted his life to the Catholic Church, places her in a delicate and morally complex position. Her determination to follow her heart takes her on a transcontinental journey from London to Australia, all under the guise of investigating a historical injustice involving a former child migrant sent to a Perth Catholic institution. This clever narrative device enables Slaney to seamlessly integrate historical awareness and social commentary into the romantic plot, adding depth to the story and enriching the reading experience.

Slaney's characterization is a standout element. Tiana is portrayed as a strong, independent heroine who navigates the tension between her privileged upbringing and the challenges of pursuing forbidden love. Her vulnerability and resilience make her relatable and engaging, while Philippe's charm and moral complexity create a captivating romantic tension that drives the narrative forward. Their interactions are tender, suspenseful, and layered with emotional stakes, making the romance feel authentic and compelling.

The novel is also beautifully atmospheric, vividly evoking the culture and social norms of the 1970s while seamlessly incorporating travel and historical context. The pacing is well-balanced, with moments of reflection and introspection interspersed with tension, suspense, and romance, keeping readers thoroughly invested in Tiana's journey.

The Heiress is perfect for readers who enjoy character-driven historical romance with rich emotional resonance and adventurous plots. Kisane Slaney delivers a captivating story of love, courage, and personal discovery, exploring the risks one takes in pursuit of the heart's deepest desires. The novel lingers with the reader, blending romance, historical intrigue, and moral complexity in a manner reminiscent of classics like Thorn Birds and Empty Cradles.

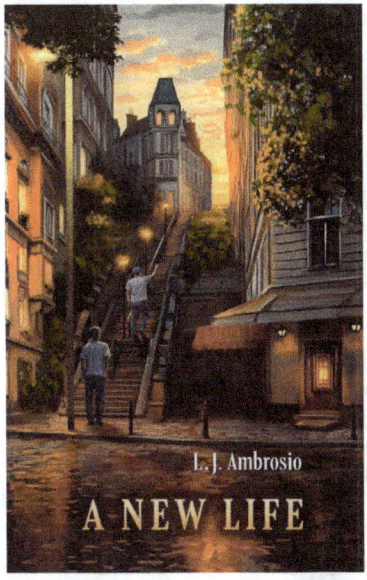

A NEW LIFE
L. J. Ambrosio

Reviewer: Jeyran Main

L. J. Ambrosio's A New Life is a tender, evocative, and profoundly moving exploration of friendship, grief, and self-discovery, set against the romantic and historic backdrop of Paris. The novel follows two close friends who leave behind the familiarity of America to confront the challenges of loss, embrace change, and pursue personal growth in a city that has long inspired artists, dreamers, and wanderers alike. Ambrosio paints Paris with such clarity and affection that the town itself emerges as a living presence—its cafés, boulevards, and quiet corners shaping and reflecting the characters' emotional journeys.

At its heart, A New Life is a profoundly human story about navigating grief and searching for meaning after devastating loss. The protagonists' journey is as much inward as outward, filled with moments of reflection, doubt, vulnerability, and courage. Their friendship becomes the steady anchor that grounds them, illustrating the profound strength of human connection in bringing clarity, comfort, and resilience. Ambrosio writes their dynamic with warmth and authenticity, avoiding sentimentality while capturing the intimacy and trust that define their bond.

The novel also delves into broader themes of resilience, love, and the possibilities of renewal. As the characters wander through the streets of Paris, they are continually confronted by memories and fears that have long lingered in their lives. Each step becomes symbolic of a deeper movement toward acceptance and healing. Ambrosio's prose is both lyrical and approachable, striking a balance between vivid description and emotional resonance. His gentle pacing allows readers to immerse themselves fully in both the setting and the characters' growth, creating a reading experience that feels reflective yet consistently engaging.

What makes A New Life especially compelling is its universality. Although rooted in Paris, the novel resonates with anyone who has faced change, endured grief, or sought a fresh start. Ambrosio demonstrates a rare ability to balance emotional depth with narrative clarity, offering a story that is poignant, relatable, and ultimately uplifting.

By its conclusion, A New Life leaves readers with more than a story of loss—it offers a testament to the human capacity for hope, friendship, and transformation. For those who enjoy character-driven contemporary fiction with emotional resonance and evocative settings, this novel is a memorable, heartfelt reminder that even after sorrow, there is always room for renewal.

ESCAPE TO THE MAROONS
Mike Weedall

Reviewer: Jeyran Main

Mike Weedall's Escape to the Maroons is a riveting historical narrative that brings to life a little-known chapter of American history: the Maroon communities of fugitive slaves who sought refuge in the Great Dismal Swamp during the late 18th century. The story follows Nathanial, an escaped slave raised as white, who is forced to flee when his identity is discovered in 1792. Barely escaping a relentless bounty hunter, he finds sanctuary among a Maroon community, where he must confront not only the suspicions of his new peers but also the complexities of embracing his true identity.

Weedall excels at combining historical authenticity with compelling storytelling. Through Nathaniel's journey, readers gain an intimate perspective on the challenges faced by Maroons: survival in one of the harshest environments in North America, the creation of self-sufficient communities, and the moral courage required to aid fellow escapees via the Underground Railroad. Nathanial's pale skin allows him to act as a conductor, ferrying freedom seekers onto ships bound for the North, a role fraught with both risk and moral complexity. These daring exploits highlight the ingenuity, resilience, and solidarity of those committed to freedom.

The novel's strength lies not only in its historical accuracy but also in its vivid characterization. Nathanial's internal struggles—accepting his identity, earning the trust of the Maroons, and navigating the constant threats from bounty hunters—are portrayed with nuance and emotional depth. Weedall carefully balances moments of tension and danger with reflections on community, loyalty, and the human drive for liberation, creating a narrative that is both educational and deeply engaging.

The Great Dismal Swamp itself becomes a character, its unforgiving terrain reflecting the resilience and ingenuity required to survive. Weedall's writing immerses readers in the harsh, yet vibrant, life of the Maroons, providing historical context while never sacrificing the emotional power of the story.

Escape to the Maroons is a must-read for those interested in American history, African diaspora studies, and stories of courage in the face of impossible odds. Weedall's novel illuminates the sacrifices and triumphs of self-liberated people, honoring their legacy while delivering a thrilling and insightful historical adventure.

LOVE & HOMEGROWN MAGIC
Patricia Bossano

Reviewer: Jeyran Main

Love & Homegrown Magic by Patricia Bossano is a heartwarming and enchanting tale that blends romance, family, and a touch of celestial magic into a story spanning seven decades and two continents. At the center of the narrative is Maggie, a woman whose life has been shaped by careful planning, a sense of responsibility, and an unwavering dedication to her family. Bossano crafts a heroine who is both relatable and inspiring—Maggie is practical, loving, and deeply aware of her obligations, yet she is not immune to the unexpected pull of love and destiny.

The novel's magic is subtle, interwoven into the story through metaphors of stardust, gardens, and the mystical timing of blue moons. These elements enhance the narrative without overpowering it, giving the story a whimsical, lyrical quality. Maggie's magical garden, where thorns and blossoms coexist, mirrors the complexities of her life—love, loss, and family obligations—offering readers a rich and symbolic setting that deepens the emotional resonance of the story.

Bossano's exploration of love is nuanced and multifaceted. Maggie's journey is not only about romance; it is about the choices that define who we are, the sacrifices made for family, and the courage to embrace the unexpected. Two loves, seemingly blessed by the stars, challenge her carefully constructed life, compelling her to follow her heart while staying true to her sense of duty. The emotional depth of these relationships is complemented by the novel's multi-generational narrative, which traces Maggie's growth and evolution over the course of decades, offering a satisfying sense of continuity and perspective.

The writing is elegant and evocative, striking a balance between lyrical prose and clear storytelling that keeps readers engaged. Themes of love, family, destiny, and personal growth are thoughtfully intertwined, making the novel both entertaining and reflective. Bossano and editor Kelsey E. Gerard succeed in creating a story that feels intimate and timeless, inviting readers to linger in its magical atmosphere long after the final page.

Love & Homegrown Magic is ideal for fans of multi-generational romance, literary fiction with a touch of whimsy, and stories where love and destiny intertwine. It is a magical, heartfelt journey that celebrates family, choices, and the enduring power of the heart.

LET BIRDS FLY
Rhea Thomas

Reviewer: Jeyran Main

Rhea Thomas' Let Birds Fly is a captivating collection of fifteen short stories that blends magical realism with poignant explorations of self-discovery and personal growth. The stories are loosely connected through the fictional company Ripple Media, providing the collection with a subtle thread of cohesion; yet, each tale stands on its own, offering unique characters, dilemmas, and magical interventions. Thomas skillfully combines whimsy and wonder with relatable human struggles, creating narratives that are both imaginative and emotionally resonant.

At the heart of the collection is the theme of finding purpose. Each protagonist faces challenges that range from the everyday to the extraordinary, yet through a touch of magic, they gain insight into their lives, uncover hidden strengths, or find the courage to make bold choices. In Flight of the Blue Fairy, Julia discovers a zipper down her back, allowing her to shed her old skin—a metaphor for transformation and personal reinvention. In The Third Eye, Sam experiences the sudden opening of a mystical third eye at a restaurant event, leading him to new awareness and understanding. Meanwhile, To the Fairest places young law student Sophia in the center of mythic attention when a golden apple attracts three competing Greek goddesses, blending classical mythology with the modern world in a playful yet thought-provoking narrative.

Thomas' writing shines in its balance of magical elements with grounded emotional stakes. The surreal occurrences in each story serve not as mere spectacle but as catalysts for reflection, growth, and self-realization. Characters grapple with identity, ambition, love, and morality, and through the magical frameworks, readers witness their evolution in a way that feels both enchanting and authentic.

The collection's pacing is deliberate yet engaging, with stories that are concise but packed with symbolism, humor, and insight. Thomas's use of magical realism enables the collection to explore complex human experiences in creative and unexpected ways, making the reading experience immersive and thought-provoking.

Let Birds Fly is perfect for readers who enjoy imaginative storytelling, magical realism, and character-driven narratives. Rhea Thomas crafts a collection that is both whimsical and meaningful, revealing the transformative power of magic, self-reflection, and courage in the quest to find one's true purpose.

TWO PEAS IN A POD
Rick S. Sulik

Reviewer: Jeyran Main

Rick S. Sulik's Two Peas in a Pod is a gripping psychological thriller that delivers suspense, tension, and edge-of-your-seat action from the very first page. The story centers on a seemingly ordinary backyard scene that quickly descends into a harrowing confrontation, showcasing Sulik's ability to transform everyday settings into arenas of danger and dread. Through precise, vivid prose, readers are immediately thrust into a life-or-death scenario, where the stakes are high, and every moment is laden with suspense.

The novel excels at building tension through carefully crafted scenes of stalking, threat, and sudden violence. The opening sequence, where the protagonist is attacked while tending to her Dogwood tree, exemplifies Sulik's skill in creating intense, immersive moments. The narrative captures both the physical struggle and the psychological impact of the encounter, allowing readers to feel the fear, desperation, and split-second thinking that define a life-or-death confrontation. The inclusion of the mother's apparition adds a haunting, almost supernatural element, heightening the emotional intensity while underscoring themes of protection, loss, and memory.

Sulik's writing is notable for its pacing and suspenseful structure. Short, sharp sentences and detailed action sequences maintain an unrelenting sense of urgency, while moments of reflection and supernatural interludes provide depth and emotional resonance. The portrayal of the assailant as both cunning and physically overpowering creates a formidable antagonist, raising the stakes and keeping readers on edge throughout the narrative.

Two Peas in a Pod also explores themes of survival, courage, and the enduring bond between mother and daughter. While the story is dark and intense, the emotional undercurrents provide balance, creating a thriller that is not only thrilling but also emotionally engaging. Sulik's ability to combine high-stakes action with rich character insight makes this novel compelling for fans of suspense and psychological thrillers alike.

Two Peas in a Pod is a taut, suspenseful thriller that delivers both heart-pounding action and emotional depth. Rick S. Sulik crafts a story that keeps readers captivated until the very last page, exploring fear, resilience, and the lengths one will go to survive

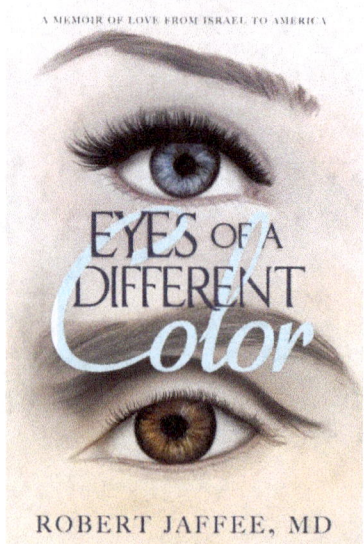

EYES OF A DIFFERENT COLOR
Robert Jaffee

Reviewer: Jeyran Main

Robert Jaffee's Eyes of a Different Color is a tender and evocative memoir that chronicles the extraordinary love story of Iris, an 18-year-old Israeli woman, and Bob, a newly minted American physician. Their romance begins in 1979 during a brief encounter, but the impulsive decision to marry sets the stage for a life of cultural adjustment, emotional growth, and shared triumphs and challenges. The memoir captures the complexities of love, marriage, and self-identity against a backdrop that shifts from New York City to the hills of Jerusalem and finally to the wide-open landscapes of Odessa, Texas.

What makes this memoir particularly compelling is its intimate portrayal of the cross-cultural adjustment process. Iris, uprooted from her familiar surroundings, must navigate a new language, confront antisemitism, and endure the isolation of being far from family and friends, all while seeking to define her identity beyond the role of a physician's wife. Bob, meanwhile, faces his own challenges as he adjusts to the demands of marriage and supports his young wife through her struggles. Jaffee portrays their relationship with authenticity, capturing both the humor and heartache that accompany such a profound cultural and emotional transition.

The narrative excels in its rich depiction of place and community. From the bustling streets and skyscrapers of New York to the sacred hills of Jerusalem and the stark deserts of Texas, readers gain a vivid sense of the settings that shape Iris and Bob's experiences. The memoir also introduces a diverse cast of individuals—New Yorkers, Israelis, Texans—whose interactions highlight the contrasts in culture, tradition, and worldview that the couple must navigate.

Eyes of a Different Color is not only a story of love but also a meditation on resilience, identity, and the universal challenges of forging a life with someone from a different world. Jaffee's writing is heartfelt, evocative, and infused with humor and warmth, making readers laugh, cry, and reflect on their own experiences of family, love, and adaptation.

This memoir is a compelling read for anyone interested in cross-cultural relationships, historical personal narratives, or stories of resilience and love that transcend borders. It offers a heartfelt testament to the power of love, the challenges of adaptation, and the triumphs of building a life together in a world of cultural contrasts.

THE QARAQ AND THE MAYA FACTOR

Stephen Weinstock

Reviewer: Jeyran Main

Stephen Weinstock's The Qaraq and the Maya Factor, the second installment in the 1001: The Reincarnation Chronicles series, is a masterful blend of epic fantasy, philosophical inquiry, and intricate character-driven storytelling. Picking up after the events of The Qaraq, the novel continues to explore the lives of Sahara Fleming and her qaraq—a mystical group of intertwined souls who have shared countless past lives. In this installment, the qaraq faces a profound challenge: the Maya Factor, a Hindu concept of illusion and distraction, begins to erode their extraordinary memory of past incarnations, threatening the deep connections that have sustained them for centuries.

Weinstock's narrative excels in balancing high-concept fantasy with emotional intimacy. Sahara's struggle to retain the qaraq's memories while navigating her estranged husband's relentless attempts to rekindle their romance adds tension and depth to the story. Their chemistry is palpable, yet the novel never reduces the plot to a simple love story. Instead, Weinstock intertwines romance with existential and metaphysical questions, exploring whether the qaraq's lives are part of a grand cosmic design or merely illusions within the Maya.

One of the book's standout qualities is its worldbuilding. Weinstock seamlessly integrates elements of Arabic scholarship, reincarnation, and mystical philosophy into a contemporary setting, creating a universe that feels both expansive and deeply personal. The author's attention to the psychological and emotional dynamics of the qaraq members brings nuance to their extraordinary abilities, making the fantastical elements resonate on a human level.

The pacing of The Qaraq and the Maya Factor is deliberate yet compelling, alternating between suspenseful revelations, philosophical reflection, and moments of high emotional stakes. Weinstock's prose is both lyrical and precise, allowing readers to immerse themselves in the complexity of multiple timelines and intertwined lives without losing clarity.

Ultimately, this novel is an intellectually stimulating and emotionally rich continuation of Weinstock's genre-bending series. Fans of epic fantasy, reincarnation sagas, and intricate explorations of love, memory, and destiny will find themselves captivated by the challenges Sahara and the qaraq face. The Qaraq and the Maya Factor is a thought-provoking, imaginative, and thrilling read that solidifies Weinstock's reputation as a daring and visionary storyteller.

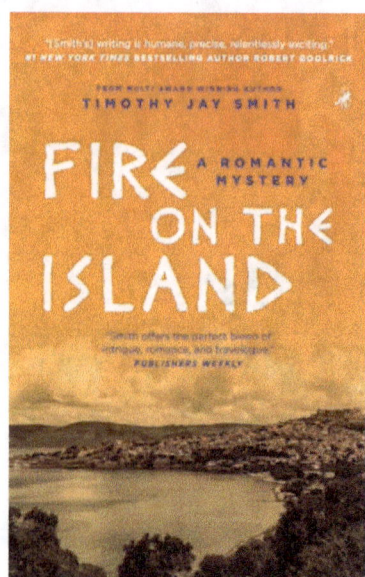

FIRE ON THE ISLAND
Timothy Jay Smith

Reviewer: Jeyran Main

Fire on the Island by Timothy Jay Smith is a gripping romantic thriller that combines suspense, intrigue, and cultural exploration against the sun-drenched backdrop of the Greek islands. The story follows FBI agent Nick Damigos, who arrives on a small island to investigate a series of mysterious fires threatening the local community. From the very first page, Smith immerses readers in the tension and danger of the situation while simultaneously highlighting the beauty, history, and complexities of contemporary Greek life.

The novel's strength lies in its multi-layered narrative. Nick's investigation reveals long-buried secrets, intergenerational conflicts, and hidden motives within the community, giving the story depth and realism. The arson plot serves as both a compelling mystery and a catalyst for character development, allowing readers to explore the intricate dynamics of village life. Smith's portrayal of the Greek setting is vivid and authentic, making the islands feel alive with sunlit landscapes, bustling tavernas, and scenic vistas, all contrasted with the ever-present tension of impending danger.

Romantic tension is another key component of the story. Nick becomes romantically entangled with a young bartender who is also his prime suspect. Their evolving relationship adds emotional complexity to the thriller, exploring themes of trust, desire, and the consequences of secrecy. Smith skillfully balances the romantic subplot with the suspenseful plot, ensuring that neither overshadows the other while maintaining a steady, engaging pace.

Beyond suspense and romance, the novel also explores social issues, including the refugee crisis and the challenges faced by tight-knit communities in contemporary Greece. These elements provide context and relevance, giving the story depth beyond the central mystery and adding layers of empathy and understanding for the characters' struggles.

Fire on the Island is a well-crafted blend of thriller, romance, and cultural exploration. Smith's vivid descriptions, compelling characters, and carefully constructed plot create an immersive reading experience that keeps the reader turning pages until the final revelation. Fans of suspenseful mysteries, character-driven romance, and novels set in evocative international locales will find this story particularly satisfying. With its mixture of tension, intrigue, and emotional resonance, Fire on the Island is both entertaining and thought-provoking, delivering a story that lingers long after the last page.